Burdens to Blessings

Seven Stories on a Journey to Wholeness

Shalonda Walker Maxie

Copyright © 2022 Shalonda Maxie

All rights reserved. No part of this publication may be reproduced, distributed, or transmitted in any form or by any means, including photocopying, recording, or other electronic or mechanical methods, without the prior written permission of the author, except in the case of brief quotations embodied in critical reviews and certain other noncommercial uses permitted by copyright law. For permission requests write to the author at the address below:

smaxievolvetbcc@gmail.com

Dedication

I give honor to my Father in heaven, the source of my strength. I pay homage to my mother Gloria Ann Walker, whose burdens birthed blessings. To my brothers Tishawn and Tony, whose burdens I share. To my ancestors who paved the way for me to be the woman I am today, thank you. To my village and mentors who nurture and love me unconditionally, I thank you. Special thanks to Change The Narrative Book Publishing Co.!

To my grandparents Allen and Camilla Walker, God rest their souls, I give thanks for their obedience. To my "mom-tie" Camilla Faye and my uncle Delbert, I thank you and I love you so very much for accepting the assignment to care for me. I am forever grateful to you and all you sacrificed to raise me. To my children Nasiria and Asir, I am forever blessed because God gave me both of you. To my husband Robert, God knew what I needed in a partner when he blessed me with you! Thank you for loving all of me.

And to every soul that connects with Burdens to Blessings, may you discover the purpose in your pain, and the blessings from your burdens.

Table of Contents

Foreword:
Elizabeth Pritchett, MD

Introduction: 9
The Woman at the Well

Chapter One: 14
Whose Child Am I?

Chapter Two: 35
Know Your Worth

Chapter Three: 55
Life After Death

Chapter Four: 76
Victim and Victims

Chapter Five: 90
Restored

Chapter Six: 105
Journey to Love

Chapter Seven: 117
Journey to Motherhood

Author's Note: 134

Foreword

*Ordained Minister and Psychiatrist
Elizabeth Pritchett, MD*

Sometimes the things that scare us the most are not the unknowns of the future, but the tangible haunts of the past. I read Burdens to Blessings with the idea of it being someone else's story. However, it didn't take long before author Shalonda Maxie's frank honesty about her life, pushed me toward a historical examination of mine. Her story is told in a deeply personal manner that is soul-baring and celebratory at the same time. And isn't that the essence of life? Trials, troubles, and triumphs float in and out of our existence in no particular order and sometimes for no apparent reason.

Jesus is recorded in the book of John saying, "I have told you these things, so that in me you may have peace. In this world you will have trouble, but take heart! I have overcome the world." (John 16;33 NIV).

Burdens to Blessings is a testament to humanity surrendered to God's Holy Spirit. It offers a pathway to emotional freedom.

    Shalonda Maxie speaks with a refreshing, sometimes painful openness about the troubles of her world (abandonment, mental illness, self-destructive behaviors, frightening medical procedures) as well as the triumphs of love gained and given. Her story reflects the truth of human existence. Burdens to Blessings lets us know that we cannot control the circumstances of our birth or the issues of our being. But we can choose to live in the triumph, rather than the trial. We can choose to embrace the beauty and celebrate the blessing rather than letting the burdens define us. Her story (or portions thereof) will resonate with many, inspire others, and will be a saving grace for some, but it will be a blessing to all.

Dr. Elizabeth Pritchett is a board-certified psychiatrist, ordained minister, and author/publisher based in Clarksville Tn. She can be found on social media @DrPsPeace or at CTNBooks.com.

Introduction:
The Woman at the Well

Have you heard of the woman at the well? She went to the well to gather water for the needs of her household during the off hours, so she could avoid the whispers, stares, and silent judgment of the other women. They filled their waterpots and talked among themselves, but never to her. Her life was fodder for the town's gossip. What people whispered about her was true. She had the unfortunate (during that time) reputation of having been divorced or widowed by five husbands and she was now living out of wedlock with a sixth man. It did not matter to the townspeople how she had come to have multiple husbands or the hurt with which she lived. I like to imagine that she treasured these quiet moments of freedom and solace that could be found at the well. But one day, when she expected to be alone, there was someone there, a man named Jesus. She was wary because it was unusual to see a man here especially a stranger. She said nothing. When he spoke she was amazed. He had not come to take something from her, as so many had done before. He had not come to reprimand her, but to speak to her heart. He spoke the truth of her life and set her free.

I have been the woman at the well. I have lived in shame. I have searched for fulfillment in the beds of men. I have tried to hide the truth of my actions because I thought it was too ugly, too sinful for those around me. I have wrestled with shame, worrying that if people knew the details of my story I would become the object of their rejection. I worry, even now, that my story will overshadow the essence of who I am and who God purposed me to be.

But I am so glad today, that Jesus came to my well, that he spoke to my heart and took my hand, spoke my truth, and set me free.

There are things in my past that I wish I could change. I wish I had had more grace, more wisdom, took more care in making decisions. I was ashamed, but Jesus has freed me from shame. I have learned that I am most free when I acknowledge my sins, accept the facts of my life, and reconcile my low moments with my personal wins. Everything I've gone through, good and bad, accomplishments and lessons learned, has created the fulfilled, whole person I am today.

So I am sharing my truth in these pages. I share my truth for my children, so that they will know my story. I share my truth with the hope that others can avoid the unnecessary mistakes of my life. I share my truth, so that others can be free in their truth. My life has been filled with both burdens and blessings. My prayer is that in these pages you will find revelation to reconcile the burdens and blessings of your life. I hope that through Jesus you can find the courage to walk in the perfected wholeness of your life!

Romans 8:28 ESV
28 And we know that for those who love God all things work together for good, for those who are called according to his purpose.

Chapter One

Whose Child Am I?

*"And the child grew and became strong;
he was filled with wisdom,
and the grace of God was on him."*
Luke 2:40 NIV

When I was a little girl, I had a friend who seemed to have the perfect five-year-old life. She had the kind of bedroom girls have on TV, a frilly pink room with a white canopy bed and flowy curtains. A life-sized dollhouse sat in the corner next to her closet full of pretty clothes, shoes, bows, and purses. Among the fun and fancy décor sat the crowning jewel of her room: the doll collection of every little girl's dream. She had Cabbage Patch dolls, Barbie dolls, and even Just Like Me dolls that cried and had real diapers we could change. The dolls came with clothes, shoes, and hair accessories to mix and match. She was my sweetest friend, her mom made the best snacks, and I loved to go to her house on Saturday afternoons. We would play "house" and she would always want to be the mom. She always said that she wanted to be a mom when she grew up and just had to be the mom every time we played together. I would always agree to the arrangement and pretend to be an aunt or sometimes even the dad. Reflecting on these moments as an adult, I think I was aware from an early age that I was a little different than most of my friends. They dreamed of being moms, but motherhood was not something that interested me. I was happy to play "house" and enjoy girly fun, but I did not feel connected to the concept of motherhood. I believe this was because my mother was largely absent from my life, and I had limited experience with what it felt like to have an involved mother.

    Many children grow up knowing their mothers on a personal, intimate level. When you are raised by your mother you know things like her smell as she tucks you in at the end of the night or the expression that she makes when her patience has worn thin for the day. You know the fold of her arm in a hug and the inflection of her voice as she calls to you from another room. Most of what I know about my mother was not learned through experience, but through bits and pieces of stories told to me over the years. I didn't have a mom; I had a

"Gloria." I knew that she gave birth to me and that I lived with her for the first few years of my life. I knew that she lived a few short miles away. I just never called her Mom. Everyone else called her Gloria, so I did too, and no one ever corrected me, not even her.

Gloria lost custody of me and my brothers when I was barely five years old; my brothers were even younger. None of us were even out of our toddler years. I don't know the ultimate reason that she was determined unable to care for us. I cannot say which incident forced my grandparents to finally intervene and take us into their home, but stories of her personality and behaviors have trickled down to me throughout the years. She was the oldest girl in her family and was often placed in charge of watching her younger siblings. My aunts have told me stories of how she would fuss at them and complain about having to be responsible for cleaning up after the younger siblings or keeping them during the summer. As she got older, she seemed to escape her life by smoking weed and partying with older men. They would hear adults' comments about her being "slow in the brain and fast in the body" or she and my grandfather fussing with each other from the other room. By the time she reached high school, my grandfather had had enough of her antics and decided to kick her out of the house.

When she was forced to take care of herself it became apparent that she was not simply a rebellious teenager, but that she struggled with mental illness. She was hospitalized for mental health issues for extended periods of time. In the eighties, Black communities had limited resources and understanding of such issues. Instead of being troubled, she was a troublemaker. Instead of being understood as emotionally unstable, she was called crazy. Instead of being referred for medication management, she self-medicated. Many of the stories I have been told about Gloria carried the same theme. She was a challenge. It was easier to wash your hands of her than to peel back the layers of partying, promiscuity, anger, and aggression that seemed to cloud many of her interactions.

Although my daily life was centered around my grandparents' house, they would take my brothers and me to visit my mother regularly. She lived in a well-known, downtown Cincinnati housing project. Four concrete buildings created a square around a dry, bare courtyard. Her unit was filled with over-worn secondhand furniture, bulging bags of clothes sat haphazardly throughout the space, and a sour smell always hung in the air. We usually visited her on Sundays after church with Kentucky Fried Chicken in the signature red and white buckets. These visits were awkward. They served as moments of clarity as to why she was considered unfit to care for us. They would begin pleasantly enough; she would pass the time with conversation laden with hope and promises that we knew were unlikely to be fulfilled. They would often end in arguments between Gloria and my grandpa. He would remind her that she needed to get herself together for our sake. She would scream that we were her kids, and he shouldn't forget it! I would watch indifferently, sunken into the tattered couch eating my chicken until Grandma would pack us up to take us home for the week.

I am not naïve to the likelihood that I didn't get the same version of Grandma and Grandpa that my mother received when she was a girl. They weren't the same people. My aunts and uncles tell me they grew softer over the years which I know came with age and their desire to protect me and my brothers from my mother's lifestyle. My everyday life at my grandparents was an opposite experience from the Sunday visits with Gloria. At my grandparents' house, I always felt loved, and I never remember going without. I would sit on my bed and play with my Raggedy Ann & Andy dolls for hours. I remember loving the neighborhood where we lived. There were always friends to play with and I loved riding my bike through the familiar streets. I loved being under my grandmother. I would stand next to her and rub the soft skin on her arm, or we would play Patty Cake. She taught me how to make simple foods, like cinnamon toast or oatmeal. I would watch her hand roll out dough for her famous yeast rolls or mix up my favorite lemon meringue pie. I always felt special with my grandparents-loved by them. I didn't have everything that I wanted, but I know I had everything I needed in my grandparents' house.

    As my grandparents grew older it became more of a challenge for them to parent three children. After my tenth birthday, they decided to send me to live with my aunt Faye and Uncle Delbert, while my two brothers were sent to live with another uncle and his new wife. This transition was a pivotal moment in my life. Aunt Faye and Uncle Delbert were active-duty soldiers and were stationed in Germany. I moved from the only neighborhood I had ever known to an entirely different country. I was especially sad to be leaving my grandparents where I got to serve as an assistant gardener, and cook, and it always felt like an endless summer vacation. Even with all these complicated feelings, still, I knew that I should not question the decision. During the Christmas break of my fifth-grade year my uncle picked me up from Ohio, and we flew to Germany. I became the oldest girl in a new household. Life felt awkward for a little while as I was not used to the strict schedule that my aunt and uncle kept, but I was quickly distracted with their new baby and my little cousin that loved to talk my ear off. With a new family to navigate and a new country to explore, I was able to settle into my new life with little drama on my part. While my aunt and uncle's house was different it still came with fun and excitement. It was nice having another girl in the house and not two rough and tumble brothers. We would always spend weekends exploring Germany or other nearby countries. Years later we moved, as my aunt and uncle were stationed in Hawaii. I experienced things and formed relationships that I would not have if I stayed in Cincinnati. My aunt and uncle cared for me as if I was their own. They made sacrifices with time, money, and love, and I did not go without in any of those areas.

    I hold the memories of my childhood close to my heart, but there were moments when I didn't feel like the other kids. I sometimes felt I missed out on the little things that other kids seemed to take for granted: calling out "Mom!" and hearing her reply, having her cook my favorite dinner, or asking her permission to go outside to play- even being mad at her for not letting me have my way. I have one memory that always stands out to me: my first middle school dance. It was so exciting. It was only a middle school homecoming, but it felt like prom to me! All the girls were dressed up. It was the first time I was allowed to wear make-up, and I felt beautiful. But as everyone else's parents gushed and shared in our excitement, I had a clear feeling that one thing was missing: my mother.

    I used to believe that not having Gloria in my life made me inadequate. I did not live with her and never knew my father. It was easy to believe that I got the short end of the stick in life. It was easy to believe that not having parents pushed me to the outskirts of society. Even in my twenties when I thought I had grown past this issue I found myself grasping for her mothering. She suddenly fell ill with cancer and the doctors gave her a few months to live, so I tried to reconnect with her. I hoped to make up for the lost years between us and missed bonding opportunities. I thought those last few months she was gifted would be a chance to redeem all that I thought that I had lost and repair my insecurities.

    As I began to heal the Lord gave me a revelation about my life that set me free. I did not have a traditional mother in my life, but I have been mothered more than I could have asked for. My grandparents had hearts open enough to take me and my brothers during their retirement years. My grandmother taught me how to cook and encouraged my loving personality. One of my aunts taught me how to always present my best self, and another introduced me to my passion as a beautician. My grandfather encouraged me to be confident and proud of who I was when I looked in the mirror, and my uncle always pushed me to set a standard for myself. Because of my family, I have never lacked anything. I have lived in nice homes and experienced cultures all over the world. I have been parented, advised, and supported beyond measure. The Lord has blessed me with girlfriends and mentors that inspire me, support me, and pray with me. I can now see that God was preparing me for a future I could have never imagined. I am overflowing in mothering!

    I am grateful for this new perspective in my life. It allowed me to open my heart to my mother and her struggles. I can picture her as a woman who experienced loss and not simply a lost woman. I can mourn for all the times she was not allowed to be more than her angry reputation or the times she didn't receive the medical help she needed. Although she may not have given me bedtime stories or Sunday dinners, she did not leave me empty-handed.

She birthed me into a family of loving women who were willing to pick up the baton and take on the race of my mothering. She allowed me to be cared for and loved by households that were not her own. She introduced my love of music. I know when my playlist plays, and I dance around the house- this is a little bit of joy that was gifted to me by my mother. I know my desire to fellowship with others and laugh comes from my mother. Even though she was not able to give as she desired- I know my desire to give comes from her. When I can bless others, I am grateful that the desire to do so was passed down from my mother. The revelations of what she gave me allowed me to open my heart to forgiveness and open my heart to experiences that I had once closed off for myself.

    The Lord was able to use the absence of my mother to create the ability to receive mothering in so many ways. In the absence of my father, He has stood in as a father. In the absence of a mother, He has stood in as a mother and connected me with the spirit of mothering throughout my life. I choose now to celebrate every portion of my life- the abundant and the scarce seasons- knowing that God uses every season for my good.

...constantly rejoicing in hope [because of our confidence in Christ],
steadfast *and* patient in distress, devoted to prayer [continually seeking wisdom, guidance, and strength],

Romans 12:12 AMP

Chapter Two

Know Your Worth

"For I know the plans I have for you," declares the LORD, *"plans to prosper you and not to harm you, plans to give you hope and a future."*
Jeremiah 29:11 NIV

One of the common threads in most childhoods is that adults often ask you what you want to be when you grow up. Will you be a firefighter, a teacher, or maybe an astronaut? It's a question that for many children fosters thought, passion, and the beginning of personal development. For much of my childhood, it wasn't a question I could answer. I hadn't yet found the thing that I thought I could do for the rest of my life. But when I reflect on my memories of being a little girl, it seems that the answer was always closer than I knew. One of my fondest memories with my grandmother is sitting in our kitchen as she pressed my hair. She used an old-fashioned pressing comb, the kind you heated up on the stove. I always felt so grown up when my hair was done, and I loved any extra special time that I spent with my grandmother. I also remember being forced to get a Jheri Curl because they were supposed to make your hair "easier to manage". The loosely curled "wet look" style was popular in the 80s, but has been joked about since then. I laugh about the memory now, but when I was a kid, I hated it! My dislike for the Jheri Curl unintentionally launched my first foray into doing my own hair. As an act of rebellion, when we got home from the hairdresser, I washed and straightened my hair to get rid of the curls that had been forced upon me by the adults in my life. This was a dangerous act because putting additional heat on my chemically treated style could cause major hair damage, but it was a risk I was willing to take to have the hair I wanted. Eventually, when I was in middle school my aunt began the familiar, young black girl experience of taking me to the hairdresser every two weeks. Once the visits to the salon became a regime, it did not take long for me to realize that the hair salon was my happy place. I was fascinated with everything about the salon experience. I loved the smell of the different hair sprays and oil sheens; my nose was even intrigued by the scents of the chemical relaxers. The sizzle of hair on the hot combs and curlers seemed like relaxing background music. The sounds of the grown-up women gossiping, laughing, and sharing wisdom with the younger women would inform my idea of friendships for years to come. Most of all, I loved watching hair transform from "workweek drab" or "bed head" into styles that women were proud to wear out on the town or to church. It was like the hairdresser had a superpower to lift women's self-esteem and add sway to their hips. When I saw women enter the shop in one state of mind and leave the shop empowered, I knew I had finally found my passion. I knew what I wanted to be when I grew up, a cosmetologist.

In the 90s, many a young black aspiring hairdresser dreamed of attending Dudley's Beauty College in Chicago, Illinois, and I was no different. At that time, Dudley's was the Howard University of Black hair, and I dreamed of studying with the best. I planned to finish high school, graduate with my Dudley's diploma, and enter the world of salon ownership. When you are young and an idealist, there is no reason to believe that everything you dream of will not come to pass for you. My dream didn't hit a dead end; instead, it met a slow and sneaky unraveling, like the fraying of an old shirt slowly coming undone over time. While the events probably started long before, the first notable event to the unraveling of my dream was meeting the man who would become my first husband.

I was young, 17, and still in high school. One weekend, I was walking through the mall with some friends when I saw him. He looked like he walked straight out of *Boys in the Hood* or *Menace to Society*. He had hazel eyes (which I would later find out were contacts), a curly high-top fade, the right shoes, the right clothes, and his most impressive accessory: a large gold chain with a blinged out rooster hanging from his neck. His confidence pulled me in before his words did any work. His attention focused on me from the moment he walked past. To a 17-

year-old with limited life experience, he seemed like a man who always knew exactly what he wanted, and it was clear that he wanted me. And as a 17-year-old who wanted to be wanted, we were the perfect fit. He was 21 and a soldier. He seemed to have unlimited money; he bought me whatever I wanted and whatever he wanted me to have. He was doting and treated me like I had never been treated before. He let me drive his car, so I could drive my friends around and show off what my man had. I never had to worry about making plans or what was happening next. He took care of it all: matching outfits to wear to his friend's BBQ or a new piece of jewelry that he had picked out just for me. He had all the right swag and paid all the right attention to convince me that I was the one. Looking back, I can't say specifically what it was I loved about his personality or his heart, but he showered me with gifts and attention. I felt secure, I felt loved, so what more could a girl ask for?

My aunt and uncle didn't approve. He was an adult, and I was not. He had experience with life and partners, he had an apartment, a vehicle, and the freedom of a young adult, while I was a high schooler who had yet to make her way in the world. And like a stereotypical teenager, I was more concerned about meeting the love of my life than heeding the wisdom of my elders. I moved on with the relationship believing that his assertiveness, his drive, and his influence over my life were what love looked like for a young woman who was going to be a wife.

Blinded by love, I graduated from high school (by the skin of my teeth), and instead of attending the school of my dreams, Dudley's, I ended up at a small beauty school near home, Moore Université of Hair Design. Although it was not my dream school, I still felt satisfied that I was on the right path to my dream job. The problem was that while I was working toward my cosmetology license, my boyfriend was being stationed at a new Army base and he wanted me to join him at his new duty station. While I was still trying to hang on to my original plan, he was creating a perfect plan of his own. He wanted me to join the Army so that we could be stationed together and live together. It sounded so perfect, and all I had to do was agree. Again, my family advised me against it. They wanted me to live my own life and forge my own path. But as I was now an adult, I chose to go with my boyfriend's plan, and (although I didn't realize I was doing this at the time) I chose to put his dreams and plans before my own. In my mind, his choice to plan our lives equaled love. His desire to be assertive and for me to be closer to him only spoke to his passion for me. Who was I to turn that down?

Six months later I was a newly christened soldier who had just made it through basic training. I was now a private in the United States Army and was stationed on an Army base with my boyfriend. A year after that we were husband and wife. We were in love. We were at the beginning of long careers, making good money for people our age. We were on the path that he saw for us: a young military couple with no kids, living life to the fullest. I thought I was happy. His plans for our lives were at the forefront. My salon dreams had faded to the back of my mind.

About five years into my Army career, I attended a required military leadership training school. During the training, I tore my Achilles tendon. It was extremely painful; it put me out of commission for several weeks and in a boot for several months. While this was a stressful event, it was additionally horrible timing as we were set to deploy to Iraq with our new Army unit as the tragedy of 9/11 occurred soon after I completed my training. All military bases were on lockdown or high alert. Some injuries might be intense enough to get a soldier an exemption from deployment, mine was not, especially coupled with the current state of the country. Even in a boot and using crutches, I was still considered strong enough to fulfill my role as a driver in the transportation department and support my unit and its mission. So, amid uncertainty and war, and with only one good leg, I deployed to Iraq. It seemed that in the blink of an eye I went from a young adult making her way in the world to a soldier in a war zone. It was during this time that my eyes were opened to the truth of what I had signed up for when I followed my boyfriend into the Army. I was far from home. My life was on the line because of the oath I made to my country and the promise I made to my man. Every day of living and working in Iraq, I lived in terror, and I cried myself to sleep with worry that I wouldn't come back alive. The combination of all these factors finally brought me to the point of seeing a crack in my husband's plan. I realized I made this choice for someone else- not for myself. I knew that once I made it home safely, I wanted to get out of the Army. I prayed that if I made it back home with my life intact that I would commit myself to God. In retrospect, I hate that the circumstances of my life had to become so extreme for my heart to open up to myself and God, but I am grateful that I opened my heart at all.

Once I was safe on American soil, I kept my promise to myself, and I began the process of discharging from the military. I told my husband I wanted to leave the Army; deployment to Iraq confirmed that Army life was not for me. I also began to remember my dream of owning my own salon. I knew I needed to make these changes for myself and my life, but my revelation created a rift in our marriage. It went against everything my husband had planned. He planned that we would both stay in the Army until retirement. He liked the financial security. He always managed the money and with us both being in the Army it was easy for him to manage our money, and he liked it that way. I began to see signs that maybe his behavior towards me was not love, nor were his actions those of a good partner. He liked to be in control, and I had been easy to control. He would always say things like, "If you don't like the way this boat is sailing you can get off." Early in our relationship, when he would say things like this, it never bothered me, but when I began to realize that I might not like the way our boat (his boat) was sailing, I began to hear his euphemisms in a different tone.

As I matured, I began to realize that many of my life's decisions were unconsciously made from a place of lack and I secretly longed for a picture-perfect family. Looking back at my dating choices, I was always looking for a happily forever after. I was always willing to be who my man wanted me to be because I didn't have a standard for the man himself. I was blind to the truth that I was the supporter of his dreams, but he was never the supporter of mine. God put a purpose inside of me, but I didn't recognize the value and the gifts that I was given, so I put them to the side.

If I could talk to my younger self, I would tell her that self-love should be your first love after the love of God. Supporting a man and his dreams may have some value but know that supporting yourself and your dreams has even more. Desiring a relationship should not come at the expense of your dreams. I have learned that what is meant to be is going to happen for you. In Jeremiah 29:11, God tells Jeremiah, *"For I know the plans I have for you," ... "plans to prosper you and not to harm you, plans to give you hope and a future."* The Lord was not simply speaking a blessing, but letting Jeremiah know that He (God) had placed those plans inside of Jeremiah and that Jeremiah had value. Jeremiah's worth was set by the most-high God! As Christians, we must believe, and we must know our worth! Because once you know your worth, your decisions will reflect your value.

A year after making it out of Iraq, I stepped back into a salon. Even before I was offered the stylist position, simply going to the interview excited me. Walking into the salon confirmed in my spirit that this was what I was meant to do, where I was meant to be. I realized that I felt a sense of belonging. I was finding myself again. I began to dream again. I renewed the dream of running my own salon. My experiences in the Army and the trying times of my marriage forced me to grow, but the salon was part of my destiny. I was finding my worth!

> **"Sometimes you have to forget what you feel and remember what you deserve."**
> **-Unknown**

Chapter Three

Life after Death

"Jesus turned and saw her. "Take heart, daughter," he said, "your faith has healed you." And the woman was healed at that moment."
Matthew 9:22 NIV

I have been given a death sentence more than once in my life. I know what it feels like to sit in a doctor's office and feel the world tilt on its axis. I understand what it means to have your life's dreams and plans be upended by one unexpected diagnosis. I know what it means to have your body betray you; for it to do the very thing that it isn't supposed to do. I have been told, repeatedly, that without surgery, without certain treatment, without a lifestyle change, I was heading toward death. I have been told, and believed, that I was broken.

When I received my first major diagnosis, I was devastated. I truly thought I was going to die in my twenties. Diabetes- I was familiar with its ugliness. My grandparents both died from complications of the disease. I watched my grandfather fight it. He changed his diet. He exercised. My aunts and uncles rallied around him. Then we watched him have a stroke. The doctor said it was because he wouldn't take the medication prescribed. My grandmother also lost her life to diabetes. She had what I now know are common complications of uncontrolled diabetes: nerve pain, poor circulation, and kidney disease. Before she left the earth, she had two of her toes amputated, lost kidney function, and needed 3 times per week dialysis. So, I knew about diabetes and the death it brought. It had taken two of the most important people in my life and now it was trying to take me. After years of a slim and battle-ready body, years of keeping in shape for my man and the United States Army, I could not control my weight. It became an issue with my husband, who made it clear that he no longer found me attractive and looked at me with disdain. When I would reach out to him for sympathy and support, he'd roll his eyes and ask, "what are you crying for?" He seemed to think I could just get over this if I exercised, ate better, and was stronger. Lord knows I wanted that more than anything. I exercised like a demon. I changed my diet. I forced myself to take the medication. But I was fatter, moodier, and lonelier than ever. Nothing worked. Eventually, my doctors ordered more tests. The results lead to a diagnosis of polycystic ovary syndrome (PCOS).

Weirdly, I felt slightly relieved. The PCOS explained the raging hormones. The diagnosis also solved the mystery of my weight gain, the difficulty controlling my blood sugar, and my moods. It also affected my menstrual cycle, hampered my ability to have children, and left me bloated and overweight. But maybe, I hoped, it would help my husband see that the changes in my body were not my fault.

I practically lived in the doctor's office. I longed for solutions to my health troubles, but with each visit, it seemed there were new concerns and ailments that my medical team was unable to explain. My emotions swirled around me with each new piece of information. However, as time moved on I began to feel a glimmer of relief that I was finding the answers to how to fix myself. Sadly, my small spark of hope would be short-lived. It would turn out that all my health issues were clues pointing to the true issue: Cushing Syndrome.

    After months of questions and tests, my doctor gave me the news that I never expected to hear. "Shalonda, you have a tumor on your brain. It's on your pituitary gland… you will need surgery…you're one in a million…" Their words seemed to float through a fog. I was confused and frightened by another diagnosis of a disease that I'd never heard of before that moment. The doctors explained that the tumor, Cushing syndrome, caused an overproduction of cortisol (a naturally produced stress hormone) which led to the excess fat tissue around my waist and face. We had been treating the symptoms, but the brain tumor had been the cause all along. I was numb, and someplace in my mind, already dead. I had lost my body. I had lost my husband. Now, I might lose my life.

Tears fell often and they fell hard. They fell through every doctor's appointment; they fell through every treatment. I spent three months being prepped for the surgery, getting my diabetes and hormones under control to have the best outcome during the procedure. I was scared. I was depressed. I was married, living single, fighting alone. I tried therapy but wasn't ready to look that deeply. I wasn't ready to 'do the work.' I was preoccupied with trying to keep my body alive. The mind would come later.

The day of my brain surgery arrived and, somehow, I made it there. There are no words to describe the churning I felt in the pit of my stomach. I wasn't alone; I had my family, I had friends, but it was only me on the table. It was only me with screws in my head. My head had been shaved. I felt like a horror show. I was bald, with screws and dents in my head, drugged on pain pills. Hearing the turns of the screws and feeling pressure in my head still haunts me. Despite the dread of the surgery, the operation went well, and I recovered. My hair grew back. Work modifications were lifted, and my life moved forward- husbandless, tumor-less, but forward. I took my death-defying lease on life seriously. I met new people and made new friends. I did new and different things. I did whatever I could to feel normal. I was alive.

    My surgery was in April and by August, I'd recovered enough to realize that I had to figure out how I was going to survive on my own, especially financially. Everyone I knew who had separated from the military went on to work as overseas military contractors because it was "good money". So I followed suit. I got a job as a contractor in Doha, Qatar. I was there less than a year, but it was one of the most memorable periods of my life. Although I was overseas again, I was more at peace because Qatar was not a war zone. I worked as a driver- which had been my specialty while I was enlisted in the Army. I loved chauffeuring my regular riders and being a pleasant familiar face during their daily schedules. I met lots of new people- many of whom let me flex my cosmetology skills during my off hours. I shopped, explored, and went to parties. I made lots of new friends- some of them are still close friends of mine all these years later. My contract job in the middle of the desert turned out be a pleasant hiatus from the chaos of my divorce and health concerns. For the first time in my life I enjoyed being the sole director of my schedule and my finances.

 After 8 months of working as a civilian overseas, I was unfortunately called home to attend a family funeral in Cincinnati. I had taken two weeks of bereavement leave for travel and decided to schedule my doctors' appointments while I was stateside. What I expected to be a routine check-up in between visiting with family would mark the end of my hiatus. I was diagnosed a second time. The tumor on my pituitary gland had returned. I was shocked. I thought I was on the verge of starting fresh. My contract wasn't up in Qatar. I had only packed for two weeks, but when my doctor told me the news, I knew I wasn't going back. A month later I'd received a medical exemption from work, sent for my things and was back on the operating table.

    This second surgery was not as traumatic. Maybe I was used to the idea of someone scooping out my brain. Or maybe as the church folks say, you go through the same test until you pass. Only, what was it I was supposed to learn?

When I woke up. I felt like I had cheated death. The first words out of the surgeon's mouth were "we believe we got it all." The medical team assured me that I should heal fine and be able to get back to living life just as I'd done after the first surgery. I left the hospital with my emotions running through every feeling possible. I was relieved to still have a life to live, but I was nervous and scared to live it. I took my anxieties to Clarksville, Tennessee, and moved in with my aunt and cousins who were waiting with open arms to nurse me back to health.

Once I was back on my feet, I threw myself into working and starting over again with a new sense of confidence, a new belief that I could dream again. I had built a life for myself in Qatar, so I knew I could do it again. I recommitted to my passion for hair. I added a barber's license to my cosmetology license and rented a booth at a popular salon. I'd survived two brain surgeries. I'd survived a divorce. I was building a business and a life. Life felt normal. I began dating again. I started therapy to work through my past hurts. My family continued to support me. I began to make new friends and build a new circle. I was even getting a growing reputation for being the life of the party.

Over time I noticed that I felt unwell more often than not. My job required me to stand for long hours. Tasks I used to complete with ease now left me weak and dizzy. I secretly worried that could no longer take the long hours standing at the salon, but I continued to press on as it was my income. After I found myself limiting my clients, so I could rest I finally crossed my fingers and went in for a check-up. After suffering in silence with my symptoms for so long I wasn't surprised to hear that the tumor had grown back a third time. Perhaps I was losing my mind because I wanted to be devasted, but I wasn't. I had been in this dark place before.

  This time the surgery was different. They removed half of my pituitary gland so that the tumor wouldn't have anything to grow back on to. My third recovery was long and hard. I struggled with low energy and low motivation. Depression engulfed me. I wanted to be alone, just me and all my diagnoses. This included the new one triggered by removing my pituitary gland: diabetes insipid, which causes salt and water imbalance. I was always thirsty and always in and out of the bathroom. My doctors regularly reminded me to keep up with my medications to stay healthy. My family encouraged me to celebrate the fact that I was alive. But spending my days managing medications and living in fear was not the life I wanted.

More and more, I began to look for my answers in the Word of God. I always identified with the story of the woman who touched the hem of Jesus' garment. She bled for years and tried every solution she could think of with no results. One day she heard Jesus was in town and went to where he was speaking, many people surrounded Him. She finally found healing by touching the hem of his garment. I understood her feelings of helplessness. I understood the years of going from doctor to doctor for help. I understood the loss and weakness she must have felt. But even more, I understood her hope that life had to be more than loss and sickness and disease. The key to her healing was her faith. She held on to her belief that life must hold more than the ugliness she had experienced. I had that same glimmer of hope. A small part of me knew that wholeness was available to me.

As I moved forward in my spiritual and health journey, I connected with a business called Head 2 Toe Change. Their mission was to provide holistic diet and nutrition counseling. They educated and supported consistent lifestyle changes to promote the healthiest life possible. I knew that this connection was the next step to walking in my wholeness. I learned how the foods I ate truly contributed to my daily health. I committed to being my number one advocate. I realized that while I thought I was at the mercy of my body, in truth I held the reigns to my life. Through diet and working with my medical team, I was empowered to live my life abundantly. I kept my health at the forefront of my prayer life and shared my story with those who were looking for a change. Sometimes my doctors resisted my extended questions, and sometimes I endured teasing from loved ones about my strict diet changes. But we all celebrated when my lab tests reported lower blood sugar and blood pressure numbers. I knew I had a tighter grasp on my health than I ever had before, and I could feel my faith in God rising.

I can boast today that I am a living miracle. I have survived three brain surgeries and too many diagnoses to name. The road to survival was long, and hard, with miles of land mines that could have taken me out at any turn. I am still walking the journey, but I am alive and living abundantly. I realized that God wanted me here and kept me here. He gave me a vision for my health and taught me to lean on Him. My question about what was I supposed to learn had been answered. My life lessons, in health, and love boil down to this: have faith in God. Let Him into every area of your life. His presence in my diet choices, my medication management, and my meditation time is the true definition of holistic healing. Seek Him in every area of your life. Life gave me a death sentence, over and again. But over and again, my God gave me life.

"If there is no struggle, there is no progress."

~Frederick Douglas

Chapter Four

Victim and Victims

"*13* Not many days later, the younger son gathered all he had and took a journey into a far country, and there he squandered his property in reckless living."
Luke 15:13 NIV

I woke up one morning and no longer recognized myself in the mirror. It was like the world had been hit by an atomic bomb, and I was the only casualty. Have you seen those action movies when the building blows up and you see the hero walking away from the rubble without a scratch wearing a pair of cool shades? Well, that wasn't me. Picture me in the piles of rubble, clawing for my life. When I look back on that period of my life, it's a miracle that I survived. But, even amid my devastation, the world continued to turn. Co-workers continued to work. Babies continued to be born. I was expected to find my footing and hop back onto the carousel of life. In the space of one year, I went from a young twenty-something wife trying to realize her dreams, to a woman struggling with her health and trying to pick up the pieces after a marriage gone bad.

    I had been a good wife. A doting wife. I deferred to my husband's guidance in all matters. I thought of him as my soul mate, my knight in shining armor. He was my first everything- love, relationship, sexual experience. How could I question the man that changed my life? If he said it was right for our marriage I believed it had to be right for our marriage. My friends thought he was controlling, but I thought that he was simply fulfilling the role of the head of our house. When he had me hand over all my earnings every week it was ok, because we had beautiful homes that his money management created. When he encouraged me to work out twice a day because my weight was climbing, I was ok with it, because I knew health and image were important to him. Through the months of doctor appointments, tests, and treatments, I was alone. I was trapped in doctor's offices, or at home trying to figure out my next steps. Through it all, my husband was indifferent. He blamed my fatigue and continuing weight gain on my laziness or lack of discipline. I was hurt and felt distant from him, but I continued to try to meet his expectations.

One day my husband forgot his cell phone at home. It rang incessantly most of the day. I ignored it at first, but I finally answered the call. There was the voice of a woman on the line. The exchange was short and revealing:

Me: "Hello?"

Her: "Who is this?"

Me: "Uhhh, you called me. Who are you looking for?"

Her: "I am looking for him. Who are you?"

Me: "I am his wife!"

Her: "Oh! I didn't know he was married. We are dating."

Sadly, that phone call opened Pandora's box full of women with whom he had been cheating. He had been "living single" while I was embodying the role of a virtuous wife. When confronted, he was unrepentant. I was stunned. At that moment I was forced to reconcile the marriage I believed we had with the truth that lay in front of me. We had just built a home together from the ground up, and that felt like forever to me. The truth was overwhelming and devastating. I wanted to fight somebody, something. I wanted to fight for the fantasy, the relationship, for what could be. However, my husband was not interested in fighting for the relationship or me. Human nature took over; unable to fight, I chose flight. I ran.

I ran two states away to my family and friends. I let him have the houses and cars. I forfeited anything that reminded me about the ten years of marriage. I left the new career I was building for myself, the healthy body that I was fighting for.

If I could turn back the hands of time, I would tell my brokenhearted, broken self that she didn't have to choose between fight or flight. I would tell her to choose rest. Today, I know that all things work together for the good of them that love the Lord. Today, I see that

God was offering me an opportunity to be alone and to spend time with Him. The loss of my marriage and my health was also an opportunity to spend time with myself and gain an understanding of who I was becoming. But I was immature. I didn't have the spiritual capacity to understand the season that was before me.

So, I ran to men. I ran to partying. I began to go to the club multiple times a week. I loved the drinking. I loved the freedom of going out when I wanted, without accountability. In my mind I was making new friends, starting life anew, and having the fun I missed as a twenty-something wife. I was hiding the pain of everything that had been torn from me with liquor and laughs. A twenty-seven-year-old woman was not supposed to be broken. I was not supposed to be divorced or diagnosed with a life-changing health issue. Brain surgery was something that affected people in documentaries or TV dramas, not me! I was supposed to be young, and vibrant and that is what I thought I was choosing to be.

    As much as I loved drinking and partying- I loved the attention most of all. I had gained 100 pounds due to side effects from my tumor and surgery. My heart was still hurting from the disillusion of my marriage. My self-esteem was through the floor. I did not like who I was during that time. I did not know who I was during that time. However, the attention from men made me feel loved and wanted. Whether it was for one night, a friend with benefits, or a budding new relationship- these men filled my tank for a moment. I ate up the compliments. I made sure I kept my look fresh and kept my clothes sexy. I was proud to have the nickname "Foxy Brown." The attention soothed the pain and kept me from having to do the work of repairing my own soul.

After the excitement of the one-night stands wore off, I became a serial monogamist. I jumped into relationships quickly and fell hard. The men were always charming in the beginning. They were handsome. They would make me laugh. The honeymoon phase was fun and felt perfect. Each time, I thought that I had found the one, and I would give my all to the relationship. I moved in with a man more than once. I chased love. I treated every relationship like a marriage because that was the only kind of relationship I knew.

No matter how much I committed to my relationships, they always followed the same pattern. They would begin on a quick high and then as the "goo-goo" eyes began to fade, I would see the cracks in the handsome, funny armor that they initially presented to me. Anger issues would begin to appear. Hidden resentment toward women would begin to make itself known during arguments. Their inability or unwillingness to deal with my health issues would arise. I even had relationships melt down into police-involved domestic violence. Looking back, I know that I was using them as tools to ignore my pain. I was a victim. I had been wounded by life and instead of taking the necessary steps toward healing, I found other victims to bring into my story. They were already broken in their own ways, also living through their unresolved traumas. I further victimized them using them for my blind desires.

    Eventually, my eyes would be opened. I would slowly begin to do the work needed to restore my soul. I would begin praying for a man who had the qualities I knew I needed in a relationship. I had already experienced a marriage that met all my material needs. I lived through a marriage that looked good on the outside. I knew I needed to focus on a person who was good for me on the inside- in his character, his goals, his choices. I wanted someone who understood my medical needs. Someone who understood that neither of us was perfect, but that we could grow together.

    I am grateful that though I was victimized, I was also rescued. Some of the wounds of life happened to me, and in some cases, I wounded myself. But no matter how I was hurt, I was saved by God who urged me to grow in my prayer life and church. My friends sometimes tease me that I went from "Foxy Brown" to "Kirk Franklin". Ultimately, I am grateful that I stepped up to be the hero in my own story. Although it happened slowly, I began to recognize the negative patterns in my life. I began to see how I was running from my pain instead of choosing to heal. In Luke 15, Jesus teaches a famous parable about the prodigal son. Instead of waiting for his inheritance, he requested it early and his request was granted.

> "There was once a man who had two sons. The younger said to his father, 'Father, I want right now what's coming

to me.' "So the father divided the property between them. It wasn't long before the younger son packed his bags and left for a distant country. There, undisciplined and dissipated, he wasted everything he had.

I'm going back to my father. I'll say to him, Father, I've sinned against God, I've sinned before you; I don't deserve to be called your son. Take me on as a hired hand.' He got right up and went home to his father.

"When he was still a long way off, his father saw him. His heart pounding, he ran out, embraced him, and kissed him. He called out, We're going to feast! We're going to have a wonderful time! My son is here—given up for dead and now alive! Given up for lost and now found!' (excerpts from Luke 15:11-21 The Message Bible)

Just like the prodigal son, when I ran from the ruins of my marriage instead of waiting and working on myself, I tried to create the life I thought I deserved. Much like the prodigal son I immaturely squandered my time and the blessing that I had been given. Just like the prodigal son, I chose to do the work of maturing, and, I too, was welcomed whole into my Father's arms.

I am learning every day to allow the space between where I am and where I want to be to inspire me and not terrify me.

Trace Ellis Ross

Chapter Five

Restored

"So if the Son sets you free you are truly free."
John 8:36 NLT

Mental health is, sadly, a taboo topic. Checking yourself into a mental hospital for treatment of depression is rarely received like checking into the hospital for treatment of a brain tumor. One gets sympathy, and the other the side-eye. No one wants to hear whispers of "crazy" or "break down" behind their back. There is plenty of pity and shame available when you share your mental weaknesses, but understanding and support are scarce. However, when I examine the life of my mother and her loneliness, when I look at the years that I lost to heartbreak and searching for myself, I know there is no price that you can put on your mental health. There are no strings or shame attached to true peace and wholeness.

    The journey of my life-my lost mother, my broken marriage, and my brain tumor, had left me at the bottom of the pits of life. Instead of braving the climb back to the top, I wallowed. The average person would not know that I was in the pits of depression, running from my own story. My wallowing was disguised as fun-men, alcohol, and parties. But I still hadn't hit rock bottom. I took risks in many different ways, but one was drunk driving. I would argue with my friends when they tried to take the keys from me. Even after drinking all night I believed that I had enough clarity to drive. In retrospect, it was only by the grace of God that I had not caused an accident or been arrested. I had been pulled over by the police numerous times for drinking. Each time I was stopped, I was able to slide my way out of any trouble by using different excuses: friends, my health, or other stories I fabricated on the spot. Once I told the officer that I worked nights and I was drowsy from a busy schedule. Another time I blamed my poor driving on my military-induced injury. By day I went to work and took care of my basic responsibilities, but when I was drinking, I was living out my alter ego.

I have learned that while alter egos may serve their purpose for a while, a person can only live a double life for so long. The truth will win out and everything you are hiding or running from will come to light. Such was the case for me. As the years moved forward- I moved forward too. I was slowly coming into myself and began to make my way up the mountain and out of the pits of life. There are many things that I would attribute to helping me climb. I was in church trying to be as involved as possible. You could find me at sunrise prayer and community service meetings. I attended all my doctor's appointments regularly and tried to follow their guidance. I was also going to therapy and confessing all my heartaches and the ways I coped with them. But I was still drinking. At the suggestion of my therapist and primary care doctor, I began seeing a substance abuse counselor, Miss Karen. She encouraged me to go to rehabilitation for alcohol abuse. Between managing my tumors and their fallout and trying to heal from emotional wounds my healthcare team agreed with her suggestion. I did not agree that I was an alcoholic, but I did agree that I had an unhealthy relationship with alcohol. Socially having a drink or two was beyond me. For me, it was a big night of partying or nothing at all. While I trusted Miss Karen and my doctors, rehab for partying seemed…extreme. I did not fully buy into the idea that it would help me move forward in my life any better than I was doing on my own.

    One Saturday, I had plans to go out with some girlfriends. My cousin was in town, and we were supposed to meet up at the club later that night. I was excited. The salon had been good to me that day. I had money in my pocket and I was looking forward to a fun night. As usual, I began drinking even before meeting up with my friends at the first stop of the night. The music was good. The crowd was perfect. I was feeling a good buzz from my signature L.I.T. During all the fun I received a text that my cousin was at another hot spot across town. I told my friends that I was heading out to meet her. As usual, my friends tried to take my keys, saying someone sober would drive me or we could meet her later. I wasn't having any of it. I had my night planned out in my head, and I wanted to keep the party going! I hopped in the car to race across town. My music was blasting. I was feeling great, making sure the party didn't stop. Then, I saw the flashing lights in my rearview mirror. Anxiety hit me as I glanced down at my dashboard. I was driving 80mph on a 45mph street. Instinctively, I knew that I was out of chances, that everything had come to a head. I didn't even try to argue with the officer. I was arrested, charged with reckless driving, and driving under the influence. I dropped from the heights of fun and freedom to the lows of truth and shame in a matter of minutes. I went from club fly to mug shot ugly all in one night.

    I felt like I had been thrown from the top of a mountain. I was so embarrassed, so ashamed. I went into hiding, locking myself in my house. I stayed in bed as much as possible. I wouldn't answer my phone no matter how much my family called. I avoided social situations as much as possible. I felt so exposed seeing my mugshot on the police website-it was as though every one of my secrets had been put on display for the world to see. When I went to court months later, I was convicted. Part of my sentence was to spend 48 hours in jail. That was my final wake-up call. It was truly one of the lowest experiences of my life. Every negative feeling I ever had about myself visited me during those two days. I felt like a disappointment. It broke my heart to think that I had broken my family's heart. I realized that my choices were only making my life worse, not better. It was a hard pill to swallow that even with all the changes I was making, my best still wasn't good enough. I had been upholding a double life that God was not in support of. The New Living Translation of James 1:8 states, "Their loyalty is divided between God and the world, and they are unstable in everything they do." I was trying to live the best of both worlds, but in truth, I was being inauthentic to the fullness God created in me. It was time for me to accept everything that God had for me. I picked up the phone to call Miss Karen and take her suggestion to go to rehab. Deciding to accept rehabilitation services was the scariest decision of my life. But it would also prove to be one of the best. First, my family breathed a collective sigh of relief. They rejoiced knowing I was going to take back the reins of my life. They supported me by paying my booth rent at the salon while I was away. I gained a little bit of peace just knowing that they were happy with my decision. When I checked in to the facility and they took my phone, I thought I would be losing my freedom, but being disconnected from the outside world allowed me to connect with myself. For 30 days I gained the gift of discipline. I was sleeping well and eating healthy meals. I began to become more aware of what was happening to my body. The facility had access to all my medical records, so the staff created a schedule for my medications. There was even a requirement for regular exercise. It was eye-opening how much a simple schedule could change my life perspective. It was also a breakthrough in my health journey to learn about healthy eating and take stock of what I truly put in my body. It was freeing to have 30 days to focus solely on myself. I discovered I was spending my time worrying about other people or trying to run from my truth. I thought I was helping, but I was only further depleting myself.

My journey through rehab ultimately taught me that I was using alcohol to cover up my hurt and pain. I was using it to run from all the things I didn't think that I was strong enough to deal with and all of the burdens that haunted me. When I chose to face what I was running from, I was much stronger than I realized. I was able to tap into all the other tools that I had in myself that I had been discounting. The parties and alcohol were tools I used for a time to serve a purpose, but now that I had made peace with my pain, they were tools I no longer needed. I could better lean on God's Word, prayer, and support from loved ones. I could better care for myself with the love I deserved.

    Completing rehab was the turning point into the next season of my life. I committed to church and made a schedule that fit my new life. I began to accept the healing that I deserved. I was able to talk about my past without resentment. I cut my hair. I spent time with different people. I was able to have fun without guilt and worship without obligation. I was able to love and be loved without insecurity. I felt different. Free.

But in the end, one needs more courage to live than to kill himself.

- Albert Camus

Chapter 6

Journey to Love

"And over all these virtues put on love, which binds them all together in perfect unity."
Colossians 3:4 NIV

Love and marriage are qualities that appear simple. When you curl up to your favorite TV show or make a quick run to the grocery store it seems as though everyone is paired off into ready-made couples. You cannot see the path that was taken to create the relationship. The stories that bind them together are invisible. Who knows what joys or tears brought them to this very moment of shopping for dinner in their neighborhood grocery store? It's not until you take the time to listen to the stories of love that you realize the finished product only appears easy. Just as the most accomplished and well-trained athlete makes it look effortless to rise to the top of their game, the happiest couple has spent countless hours behind the scenes doing the work toward the relationship that everyone sees.

When I was young and thought I knew what love looked like, I had my heart broken. Since my first husband pulled the rug from under me, I spent much of my life story focusing on my brokenness and my heartache. But, over time I have learned that even the most fragile heart can heal. If we do not run or hide but choose instead to care for and nurture our hearts, then they can not only be restored but grow. I know this is so because Psalms 147:3 says that the *Lord is close to the brokenhearted and binds up their wounds*. I have learned that though broken hearts are a part of life there is healing on the other side. Not only will you be at peace, but you will have all the wisdom and growth to take with you on the next journey of life.

I would love to tell you that I went through my healing process and found true love on the other side. But life is generally messier than we dream, and my life never seems to play out as expected. Over time, my first marriage began to fade into a distant memory. I survived two brain surgeries. I was living my childhood dream of working in a hair salon, and I was becoming a regular at church. The incessant bed-hopping and partying was no longer as fulfilling as it was in my early years of heartbreak. I was beginning to feel more settled in my new life. I was maturing and could feel myself moving into a new season. So, when my good friend insisted that we hit the bar after work, I immediately declined. It was a Tuesday night. I saw no need to go out and have a drink in the middle of the work week, but she was persistent. I reluctantly agreed to join her. I was still in my work clothes when we walked into the virtually empty building. We sat down at a table, and I was already ready to leave. Just as she was about to head to the dance floor, a friend of hers walked up and she quickly introduced us as she walked away from the table. His name was Robert, and they were childhood friends. He was there in the middle of the week because it was his birthday, and his friends wanted to take him out. It turned out we were two people who were pressured into going to the bar on a Tuesday night. I bought him a birthday drink and we talked.

    Despite being strangers our conversation was surprisingly easy. We discussed what each of us did for work. We laughed about the fact that we had both been dragged out by friends on a Tuesday night. He told me about his young daughter and how he and her mother broke off the relationship but were co-parenting well. I shared with him my health issues and how they had given me a new perspective on life. He shared that after the ups and downs of his last relationship he was tired of dating and would prefer to be in a serious relationship. Inside my head, the wheels began to turn. I happened to be sitting at a table with a man who was saying he wanted the very same things that I had been wanting. Before I could catch myself, I blurted out "You're going to be my husband one day!" I couldn't believe it! I had broken the cardinal rule of dating. I literally met this man just two hours before and I already had us walking down the aisle. Instead of being mortified and running out of the place screaming, he laughed and asked for my number.

    We casually dated for about a year and then I abruptly stopped hearing from him. I later found out that he was dating someone else. I was disappointed, but I had gotten more involved in church and began dating other people as well, so I did not have much time to be broken-hearted. About a year later, he messaged me on Facebook wanting to see me and rekindle our relationship. I was hesitant to reply because during our time apart my personal life seemed overwhelming. I had finally decided to enter a rehabilitation facility on the recommendation of my therapist. I had also found out that my brain tumor had returned for the third time, and I would need to have yet another brain surgery. I took a while to respond to his message, but by the time I wrote back, we quickly rekindled our relationship. I met his daughter who was now three years old. We became more and more serious and eventually moved in together. His mother had some health problems, so I helped him care for her. We were a serious couple.

He did not bat an eye when I explained the details of my brain surgery. He listened while I lamented and worried about having to have the surgery for the third time. He held my hand when I cried. When I woke up from my third brain surgery, he was right there waiting for me. He cared for me and nursed me back to health. He was patient with the changes that the surgery brought about in my body. His support was everything I longed for when I was first diagnosed with my tumor a decade before. The care he provided for me now was everything that I felt robbed of from my first marriage. I know what it feels like to have a partner who is unsupportive during low times in life, so I did not take his presence for granted. I told Robert that he was my husband the first night that we met, and my words had come full circle. I had grown from a blind victim kind of love to a mature, eyes wide open partnership kind of love. We married that summer with just the two of us, my pastor, and a witness.

    I went from single girl searching to wife and mom. I knew I was with the right man, but there were family dynamics to navigate. With my new daughter came her mother and a new extended family that I had to learn how to build a connection with. Eventually, our family relationship grew into something like the Brady

Bunch, but there were some battles that we had to make it through along the way. Robert and I would also learn how to navigate being in business together. Robert's passion was cars, and we ventured into the detailing business. That too was an uphill road. Gaining clientele, managing employees, and keeping business and romance was no small feat, but we pressed forward.

 Just as the business was beginning to make a profit and we had a good reputation in the area, there was a devastating accident. My husband and stepdaughter, Nasiria were hit head-on by a speeding vehicle. They were both rushed to the hospital with multiple shattered bones and fractures. It was a miracle that my husband and bonus baby were still alive. Just as Robert had stood by me as I recovered from my final brain surgery, it was now my time to support him in sickness and in health.

    Through the "for richer or poorer and sickness and health" of our marriage, I have learned that love is truly beautiful. However, that does not mean that it is easy. Its beauty does not mean that the road to love is smooth or straight. There were many times that I could not see that I was on the right path because I was too distracted by the difficulty of the journey. Because my path has been filled with pain, heartbreak, and loss, I had to learn about true love. I had to learn how to love myself, my husband, and my new family. It was a process-a journey- one that I am still on. If you are still searching for what love looks like in your life, please take a breath and trust that you are on the path that the Lord has laid before you.

"Love makes your soul crawl out from its hiding place." - Zora Neale Hurston

Chapter 7

Chosen for Motherhood

"For many are invited, but few are chosen."
Matthew 22:14 AMP

There is an adage among parents of newborns that "sleep begets sleep." It is meant to counteract the myth that skipping naps will lead to a better night's sleep. The truth is that a baby who gets good sleep during the day will also sleep well at night. In other words, you can't have too much of a good thing, in this case, sleep. I have learned that this adage also applies to love. When you have healthy love in your life it opens the door for more love. You want to share the good things that you have with everyone around you. Love begets love. We see this often in marriage. Two people desire to expand their love in the embodiment of a new baby.

This was the case with Robert and me. In my first marriage, kids were never on the table, but with Robert things were different. Just by saying "I do" I became the bonus mom of an adorable and exuberant little girl named Nasiria, and we knew that we wanted to expand our family. Once we made the decision, we jumped in with both feet. We knew that my health issues would make getting pregnant challenging, so we saw the necessary doctors, and they prescribed the necessary hormones and regimens that we would need to follow to increase the chances that we could conceive a child. When the boxes of vitamins, supplements, and medication arrived on my doorstep, my excitement to start the process faded as quickly as it had arrived. While I knew in my heart that there was more for our family, I was not so sure that this highly regimented process was for me.

During this time, it happened that one of my cousins was going through her own parenthood journey and was expecting a child. It was an unplanned pregnancy with sensitive circumstances, and my family knew that she was unsure what her decision would be once the baby made its way into the world. Because it was a challenging situation, our family simply stayed in prayer and supported my cousin while she carried the baby. Unfortunately, by the time she gave birth, she was not in a good place emotionally, and she took some time to work on her mental health while her mother (my aunt) took home her baby boy. Her mother and sister spent a lot of time taking care of the new baby. I would help and babysit from time to time to give my aunt a break. Having a tiny, adorable, infant to snuggle regularly was great for my aunt, but horrible for my baby fever!

The months began to tick by, and my cousin still had not bounced back. She would come and love on her son on her good days. She named him Asir Cadman (Arabic for *Chosen Warrior*). We all loved him and loved on him. My aunt continued to be his primary caregiver, but she was beginning to burn out. She had raised four children of her own as well as nieces and nephews, and raising a newborn was not in her retirement plans. She was calling on me more and more to give her a break. I never turned her down, my baby fever hormones would not let me! I went from watching him so she could attend appointments so she and my uncle could have a date night, to keeping him overnight or for entire weekends. I had not yet discussed with Robert the strong feelings and thoughts I was having about Asir, and over time he began to ask questions about why Asir was always at our house. When he would come home from work, we would already be settled in on the couch watching our favorite tv show. I could not blame him for his hesitancy though; neither one of us was expecting to have a new baby in our home so regularly nor so soon.

    By the time Asir turned four months old, he was pretty much a resident of our home. It had become clear that my aunt was more than willing to be a grandmother, but she was not ready to raise another child. My cousin was still battling postpartum depression and not mentally ready to parent full time. With the support of her mother and the rest of our family, she made the difficult decision to give custody over to us. I was content with spending most of my time caring for my new cousin. The love surrounding Asir made me completely happy. Even Robert was slowly accepting a newborn in the house. One afternoon I woke up from a nap to find baby Asir cuddled in Robert's arms and I instinctively knew that this temporary addition to our household had become permanent.

During this season of my life, I felt like I was exactly where I was supposed to be. It seemed like my life had come full circle. All the ups and downs of my life had brought me to this very moment. My family had taken me in as a child when my mother was ill and unable to care for me, and now, here I was, able to do the same for a loved one. It was not only my desire but my opportunity to repay the universe! I felt at peace. In many ways, I was in awe. I felt that if carrying a child never happened for me then I would still be ok because I was where I was supposed to be in life.

    We often think that when we find our purpose, the journey of our lives will magically become easy. I have found that finding purpose simply means that you have found the tools to handle what is to come on your journey. Initially, all was well in new mommy land. My cousin was happy that her child was in a loving home. She was able to see him when she wanted and still take care of herself. Her visits were pleasant. She seemed at peace with her decision and encouraged me to be at peace with my mommy role. She even encouraged little Asir to call me mommy. Any guilt that I had about her not being able to mother her own child was wiped away by the fact that everything seemed to be falling so perfectly in place. Until it wasn't.

Over time, my cousin's visits to see Asir became more sporadic and erratic. We never knew what mood or behaviors to expect when she would arrive. Would our visits be a relaxing Sunday afternoon, or would she ring the doorbell at midnight with a couple of friends in tow demanding to see Asir? I was growing increasingly worried about her changing behavior, and my husband's patience with the situation was growing shorter by the day. My feelings were all over the place. This was my sister-cousin whom I loved and who I recognized was struggling to make her way through this open adoption. How could I judge her behavior -especially when I was the child of a mother who struggled with such a similar story? It was through this turmoil that I was pushed to confront what it really meant to be a mother. Though I loved my cousin, and though I wrestled to reconcile my own childhood with Asir's, if I was going to be his mother then I had to decide what was best for him, no matter who it offended. He was a baby who deserved a peaceful life and a schedule. It was not fair to him for anyone to randomly show up without care and concern for our household. I implemented guidelines and a schedule for her visits. This was the first hard decision I had to make in my mother role. It created tension in my relationship with my sister-cousin, and some of our family members felt they had to pick sides. This hurt me, but I learned that despite what I saw on the TV screen, being a mother does not always feel good to the soul. Motherhood requires sacrifice, it means taking hits- sometimes to our own ego and desires. I learned that if I really wanted this job that I believed God saved for me, then I would have to sometimes make the hard decision.

From the outside looking in, I saw the love and cuddles of motherhood. I saw the cooking and family movie nights. What I did not see was the growth and maturity required to shape a child for the world. My cousins tease me because they say I used to be the fun cousin and the cool auntie, but now that I have a family of my own, I walk the straight and narrow! I laugh too because it's true. I have received a revelation of the importance of motherhood that I did not have when my world focus was only on myself. Motherhood is my personal contribution to the future of the world.

It is in part the reason that I chose to write my story. I want my children to read these words and learn without all the heartache that I had to experience to get to the freedom that I have today. I am committed to the responsibility of teaching our children about loving themselves, loving God, and preparing them for the world. I am committed to surrounding them with a village beyond our household. I am a bonus mom, and I have the privilege of being part of a village to my daughter from another mother. I want them to know that I am not the center of the universe and others in this world can support them as well.

Parenting is a heavy assignment, but it is not without rewards. I find joy in knowing that God trusts me enough to do the work. I find joy in the decision my cousin made to trust me to mother her son, even if one of the consequences of that decision has been the ever-changing dynamics of our relationship. I find joy in the wonder that mothering comes in so many forms and not simply the ways we expect. I am rewarded to see my son's firsts: his first steps and words, his first day at school, and his first T-ball game. I get to curl up on the couch and listen to the pure wisdom of a pre-teen daughter and see the world through her eyes. I feel joy in those moments when my children hug me and tell me they love me or say thank you out of the blue. It is a gift to watch children grow and mature, a gift to see the fruit of everything that they are taught.

If I am honest, I still deal with "what ifs" surrounding my relationship with my mother. I still wonder who or what I might have been if she'd had the mental health interventions she needed at a young age. I struggle with my role in keeping Asir connected to his mother. How much of their relationship should be a burden on me? I still sometimes grieve the loss of the sister-cousin relationship I had before I walked into motherhood. I acknowledge that I have not come full circle with my mother story, but I know that I am walking the circle to its completion. Although I did not have a mother in the traditional sense, I am living proof that motherhood exists in many ways and in many forms. God's love is not limited to traditional families or cookie-cutter households; my life story is proof of this. I believe that because of my unique story, I was chosen to be a mother in a unique way.

> **Mother [mu*th*-er]** *noun*
> ***1. A person who loves unconditionally, the maker and keeper of precious memories, a***

person much loved and greatly admired.

Author's Note

Thank you for taking the time to read my story. The truth is that there is so much more that I could have shared with you; there are many more blessings and burdens that I have lived through. There are many more stories of my own and others that intertwine with mine that I did not share in the pages of this book. While the stories may vary in their nature, their joy, or their pain they all share the same thread of bringing me closer to the Shalonda who God has been calling me to be all along.

I pray that this book is a reminder that you never know the truth of a person's life until they choose to share it. I have learned it is much easier to look put together on the outside than it is to be put together on the inside. While society would have you think you simply need to buy an outfit or have a certain car, the truth is there is no magic antidote to the perfect life. As a cosmetologist, I know that you can change your hair, lashes, and even body to suit your latest whim, but you will carry your soul with you everywhere you go. So, know that you are not alone in the burdens of life. No matter how low your problems or your secret place lie, I have been there. But more importantly, God found me there and He will meet you in your low places as well.

  My story is not over. I am still on my journey. I am accepting that I am who God created me to be, unapologetically. I am accepting the strength to do the hard things that come with my life, and I am accepting the peace that comes when I do not resist the Lord's plan. I hope that my story will help you to do the inside work because your willingness to fight is what keeps you in the game. I can testify that once Christ is your foundation, all roads will lead you back to Him.

 Finally, my prayer is that the words in these pages will spark a flame that will encourage you to go through your go-through because there is love on the other side. There is purpose on the other side. We may often get stuck in the burdens, but there are blessings on the other side.

Peace and Blessings,

Shalonda Maxie

Burdens to Blessings is an underdog story for the saint and the sinner! A collection of stories that exemplify the life of an overcomer Shalonda Maxie's life will surprise you, pull at your heartstrings, and then leave you cheering for the win. From a humble childhood in Cincinnati, Ohio to serving in a war zone in Iraq her spiritual journey will push you to reflect on the way you view your own trials. Her heartache will move you to tears. Her encouragement will make you want to share this story with a friend.

Shalonda Maxie is a Veteran of the United States Army, who served in the Iraq War. She is a certified peer support counselor, a licensed cosmetologist, and a faithful intercessor, but her proudest accomplishment is that of Wife and Mother.

Made in the USA
Columbia, SC
03 August 2023